ANGELS, ANARCHISTS & GODS

CHRISTOPHER FELVER

LOUISIANA STATE UNIVERSITY PRESS

Baton Rouge and London

MASTER PRINTS: Kirk Anspach
PHOTO EDITOR: Marilla Pearsall
ART DIRECTOR: Laura Gleason
PHOTOGRAPHIC SUPPORT: Alex Ivanov, Rodney Phillips, Rita Bottoms, Tom Scott,
    Bernard Mindich, Jim Szalapski, Jack Darrow, Dennis Herne, Bob Dawson, Ellen
    Manchester, Jerry Grossman (Nikon)
TYPEFACE: display: Minstrel, Helvetica; text: Helvetica
PRINTER AND BINDER: Everbest Printing Co. through Four Colour Imports, Ltd.,
    Louisville, Kentucky

Library of Congress Cataloging-in-Publication Data:
Felver, Christopher, 1946–
    Angels, anarchists & gods / Christopher Felver.
        p.   cm.
    ISBN 0-8071-2085-5
    1. Celebrities—Portraits. 2. Portrait photography. 3. Felver,
    Christopher, 1946– . I. Title.
    TR681.F3F45 1996
    779' .2'092—dc20   95-26432
                                                             CIP

CONTENTS

Felver's Faces   ix

Containing Multitudes   xi

Photographs   1

Gregory Corso's Poem   205

Index of Photographs   207

I thank each artist for the gift of courage and inspiration which is the heart and soul of this book. I celebrate the myriad nuances in the voice of their human faces: sometimes humans in trouble, sometimes in delight.

FELVER'S FACES

Robert Creeley

Here are two facts of remarkable poignance: the unique power of a photograph to evoke "a cigarette that bears a lipstick's traces," and now all these images of dreamers and friends from a past fading all too quickly. Back of all the layers and echoes of subsequent events, like they say, theirs was the bedrock company made a human presence that still can move the heart in the most unexpected way. Is it the painful admiration we Americans have for the outcast, the marginal, the *fellahin* as Amiri Baraka called them? Is there a sense that theirs was a kind of happiness we'll never know?

Always in Christopher Felver's portraits the subject seems altogether open to being seen and is, in fact, both intimate and comfortable, often welcoming. In this way Felver's art comes close to his people. He has no interest in a specious objectivity nor is there a dogmatic judgment, too often met with in such an undertaking, blurring all it sees. There is no contest here, rather a delight that looks both ways. How else would John Wieners, for one, ever be at home in such a "place," or Gregory Corso be utterly the complex power of person he truly is? Beyond whatever we might say of these two great poets of a timeless moment, here they stand or sit or look out at us still with eyes of a patiently humorous, acknowledged life, neither sentimental nor quizzical. Again and again these people are at home in the place Felver finds them, either directly responsive or else with hands or body turned simply to some other preoccupation of usual kind.

Perhaps the juxtaposition of those images which are particularly casual—people together, talking, affectionate—make those which are then the singular, intensive look of these same persons all the more emphasized. It is literally haunting to see Richard Brautigan's eyes, with their humor, his slight smile, the confidence of his charming headgear. Or to feel again Abbie Hoffman's embracing, irresistible energy, his playfulness and humor. Or Allen Ginsberg so close that his head almost bends to accommodate the camera, looking in and out at one and the same time. There are so many here we can recognize as what we all of us hoped for and wanted, just to be for real, to care about the kind of world we lived in, to go for broke.

Time, of course, has its way with everyone. These dear images are already moving away toward other memories and meanings. But for these moments when each was, just so, *there,* it was Christopher Felver who saw them impeccably. He was there too.

CONTAINING MULTITUDES

Douglas Brinkley

An artist wears his work in place of
wounds. Here then is a glimpse of the sores
of my generation. Often crude, irrelevant—
but done, I can assure, with a fierce heart.

—Patti Smith

Democracy:
Catch in the throat,
that beautiful sadness.
We open the package
to wonder what the gift means.

—Ralph Adamo

Someone once said that a photographer is like a beachcomber on the shore of another's experience. Chris Felver is a beachcomber all right, only he is walking in tandem with his subjects. He is a trusted accomplice, a confidant who uses his camera to portray the human face behind the celebrated mask. The lauded friends and spontaneous acquaintances who populate this ambitious collection share a common characteristic: they are artists, writers, musicians, and public servants who believe in humanity, equality, and social fairness. None is afraid of controversy or of challenging the status quo. Each has left a distinct imprint on our world and has proven that a single voice or one direct action can, as Walt Whitman put it: "Unscrew the locks from the doors! Unscrew the doors themselves from the jambs."

Felver's affinity for the thinkers and doers of this world came to him naturally. Born in Pittsburgh on Columbus Day, 1946, Felver grew up in Akron, Ohio, the son of a trial attorney who quoted Edmund Burke at the dinner table and an actress who starred in George Abbott's *Kiss and Tell* for three years during World War II. Felver's maternal grandmother, a strong independent Irish widow, spent long stretches with the family. The household he grew up in was a combination literary salon and theatrical greenroom where art and politics flourished side by side. This talkative Irish clan debated the virtues of John Foster Dulles' diplomacy and the significance of Norman Mailer's *The White Negro,* the societal impact of *Brown* v. *The Board of Education,* and the improvisational jazz of Thelonious Monk.

Music and its diversity of expression was a crucial aspect of Felver's early life. His grandmother played Cole Porter and George Gershwin tunes nightly on the baby grand in the living room, while on CKLW AM, Detroit's "Motor City Radio," Felver became enamored with the distinctive sounds of Ray Charles and Jackie Wilson. Each year, the Felver family, along with director Arthur Lithgow, spearheaded the Great Lakes Shakespeare Festival on the back terrace of Akron's Stan Hywet Mansion. Together they cosponsored avant-garde events at the Akron Art Institute and took an activist part in local politics. When Felver was fourteen his grandmother took him by train to Washington, D.C., for John F. Kennedy's historic inauguration. "It was a defining moment for me," Felver insists. "Watching Robert Frost read 'The Gift Outright' solidified politics and art for me."

For all the artistic involvement and civic pride, there was still something sheltered about life in Akron, Ohio, in the 1950s. Ahead of its time as a more or less racially integrated, community-minded town, Akron exuded a progressive aura, due in part to organized labor. For instance, Felver, a budding young golfer, played on the racially integrated Good Park course, caddying occasionally for Cleveland Brown fullback Jim Brown. This experience belied the reality in much of the country: Jim Crow still reigned supreme south of the Mason-Dixon Line.

Calvin Trillin once suggested in *The Nation* that Akron's motto should read "Preferable to Youngstown." But to the Felvers Akron was what the word *Ohio* means in the Iroquois language: "Something Great." Felver spent his teenage years hanging out in the smoky music clubs of Akron where the Pretenders and Devo would get their New Wave starts ten years later. America's future poet laureate Rita Dove attended Felver's Buchtel High School, where she explored a poetic world made available to her by the poems of Langston Hughes, who had lived in Cleveland. Jim Jarmusch of nearby Cuyahoga Falls was at this time just starting his film career, and Ron Horning, a poet who would later publish poems and translations in *The New Yorker,* was turning Felver on to the Beat Generation writers. After one reading of Lawrence Ferlinghetti's *A Coney Island of the Mind,* Felver was ready to abandon the shackles of West Market Street.

Like so many Ohioans who have wanted to escape the Buckeye State, Felver's ultimate getaway destination was south Florida, where Akron gray was an unknown color and sleet was something one saw inside the palm tree–lawned movie theater. Taking his golf clubs and independence with him, he drove southward, in the pinewiney silence of an Appalachian night, to the art deco land of pink flamingos and relentless sun.

Greater Miami in the 1960s was a pastel-hued place of stunning contrasts: Richard Nixon's Key Biscayne retreat and a transient counterculture drug scene to rival San Francisco's. Comedian Lenny Bruce once said about the resort area that it was "where neon goes to die," but for a budding artist from the north country, it was where you went to find inspiration. Felver had earned a golf scholarship to the University of Miami, where he studied history when not on the green fairways of the Biltmore Club or in the boisterous cafés of Coconut Grove. Art held court at the Hamlet and the Gaslight. "The diversity of ideas exchanged at these saloons taught me as much as any seminar," Felver maintains. But something was beginning to taint the palm-treed paradise: the Vietnam War. "We'd hold our breath as one by one, our best friends were drafted," Felver remembers. "We'd throw a wild party as a boot camp send-off, then watch that same healthy college pal return weeks later twenty pounds thinner and exhausted. We'd throw another, more sober party and watch our newly conscripted private depart again, sometimes forever." Films became an essential diversion. Dennis Hopper and Peter Fonda's *Easy Rider* zapped his consciousness like a thunderbolt. Costa-Gavras' *Z* and Haskell Wexler's *Medium Cool* taught Felver the political power of film and the thin line separating reality from art.

As the draft lurked ever closer, Felver decided to enlist in the army to avoid it. After boot camp, he was stationed at Fitzsimmons General Hospital in Denver, where he administered to young soldiers with mangled bodies, much as Whitman did during the Civil War. It was an overwhelming and traumatic period, with Bob Dylan's "Masters of War," Barry McGuire's "Eve of Destruction," and Country Joe McDonald's "Hell No We Won't Go" directing his moral compass instead of the orders from his superior officers. After ten months, Felver was discharged as untrainable. Trading his army greens for bellbottoms, his combat boots for sneakers, Felver fled the authority of the U.S. government for the serenity of the Berkshires. He headed straight to Alice's Restaurant in Stockbridge, Massachusetts, where renegade artists from all over the country congregated to share poetry, music, and agrarian-socialist values. Felver became an integral part of the bohemian scene, strumming his hand-me-down Gibson guitar, writing songs, and reading voraciously at the Lenox Bookstore.

"Art comes into being through a chain of inspiration," critic Harold Rosenberg wrote, and Felver's journey from Stockbridge to *Angels, Anarchists & Gods* is a saga of hard work, muse encounters, and Parnassian visions. Inspired by Jack Kerouac's *On the Road* and Neal Cassady's *The First Third*, as well as the need to make a living, Felver teamed up with an Ohio chum, bought an old Ford school bus, and embarked on a road odyssey to Mexico. For a year he enjoyed the freewheeling life-style of fellaheen villages, where they would purchase Mexican crafts and clothing, returning to the States to sell their goods on college campuses. Buying and selling failed to hold Felver's interest for long. He sold his bus in Mexico for $100 and headed to Europe and the London College of Printing and Film School. It wasn't long after that he made his first photographs. "The photograph brought Art down from its pedestal and gave it to the masses," Andrei Codrescu has observed. Felver saw film and photography as a way to connect with people.

For over twenty years now, Felver has taken photographs. He has returned to old haunts to capture the spirit of friends such as Alice Brock, leaning on her Eldorado with its license plate reading ALICE B, or Arlo Guthrie in front of Alice's Church almost thirty years after the release of his satirical antiwar ballad, "Alice's Restaurant." Many of Felver's shots were taken "on the road," in the midst of the action, as with his collection of Beat photographs that "merely happened" over the years of spending time within the scene.

Sometimes a photographer can be best understood by the print he selects to display to the world. In this regard, Felver's art is a subtle insiders' game, the punch line apparent only to those familiar with art and literary circles. What better way to capture the competitive nature of the New York art scene than to show Kenneth Koch and Larry Rivers dueling in front of Rivers' looming canvas entitled *Les Misérables*? The juxtaposition of Carolyn Cassady, dressed in her London best, perched upon a motor scooter, allows us to understand her relationship with Neal Cassady in a way a written biography never could. And Toni Morrison's face, with its regal power, intersected by sunshine suggests a complex personality that may very well contain a sense of humor as well as the angry defiance we publicly know. "I am not afraid of light and shadow," Felver avows. "They are metaphors for substance."

"Photography records the gamut of feelings written on the human face," Edward Steichen commented of his own art. Felver, like Steichen, is able to realize these human feelings in their fullest form. Even when his subjects don sunglasses, there is nothing illusive about Felver's images. In fact, the portraits often portray brutal truths of life. Poet James Schuyler is found in his Chelsea Hotel apartment, surrounded by bottles and pills, ill and near death. Working on his manuscripts, he is sustained by the hope that his art will transcend his own life. Vietnam veteran Ron Kovic smiles from his wheelchair with poet Jim Carroll leaning at his shoulder. Easy lives? No. Staunch survivors? You bet.

Felver can be sly about his touchstone art; there is a hearty humor behind many of his intimate images. The pose is a collaborative effort, the subject often in delightful cahoots with the photographer. Charles Bukowski clearly understands the self-deprecating humor behind his muscle-flexing bravado in front of the Stop-and-Go beer refrigerator; Hubert Selby, Jr., is smirking with Felver as he poses on craggy Montgomery Street in San Francisco, the last exit to nowhere; Kurt Vonnegut swings his bare feet in a carefree fashion, a hybrid embodiment of his beloved Mark Twain and Huck Finn. Felver is positive "these people all understand that, apart from the tragedy in life, it's a *joie de vivre* that's essential."

Felver has another rare gift—making angels out of anarchists. Under the intense scrutiny of Felver's lens Bobby Seale and Angela Davis appear less ominous and more stately than ever before. These are not the gritty faces of urban terrorists but of wise survivors, lifelong champions of the downtrodden and oppressed. The lonely rage of the Black Panthers has fermented over the years into an emphatic, personalized compassion that was buried behind the fiery radicalism of youth. Can one doubt that the single exposure included of attorney William Kunstler, with dramatic brow and combative twinkle in his eyes, speaks volumes about his rhetorical championing of the underdog?

Many of Felver's photographs are political statements, for he is a democratic socialist imbued with a healthy dose of Catholic libertarianism. To Felver, dissent is democracy in its truest form. There is also a moral dimension to each of his frames; he treats his subjects with a spiritual grace. Felver's subjects emerge from these portraits "at ease and lighthearted," as Whitman might say, with their human dignity enhanced. Outsiders are championed here as Whitmanesque insiders, as if a Robert Rauschenberg collage or Jimmy Carter house-build or Hunter S. Thompson obituary of Nixon or a Dennis Banks "sacred run" can redeem the nation. These are not portraits taken by a cynic, but by a pervasive optimist. Jan Kerouac is not mourning at her father's Lowell graveside, she is honoring the accomplishments of his life with a knowing smile. Willem de Kooning, ravaged by Alzheimer's disease, is perched in his faithful wooden rocker staring intently into a drying canvas. He has left the world of greed, racism, and environmental degradation behind; what remains of his soul is pure creation. A hundred years from now presidents like Ronald Reagan and Bill Clinton will have faded into memory as surely as Rutherford B. Hayes and James Garfield, mere asterisks to history. Felver believes that artists such as Robert Motherwell, Frank Stella, Helen Frankenthaler, and Louise Bourgeois will always be universally relevant, even in the unimaginable distant cosmos, for their work embodies eternal truths as surely as the Grand Canyon or the Great Plains.

The musicians populating this volume are some of Felver's personal favorites. Cecil Taylor is a friend. The Fugs used Felver's *Woodstock Byrdcliffe Barn* portrait for their last album cover. Patti Smith offered Felver the transcendent pose that made Robert Mapplethorpe famous. For Felver, listening to the Zion Harmonizers is as close to God as one can get on earth. Pete Seeger is Felver's idea of the quintessential American. Singing at the Beacon Sloop Club on the Hudson River, Seeger is a veritable one-man songbook of national folk treasures. What is not revealed in the illuminating photograph of Townes Van Zandt and Ramblin' Jack Elliott is that Felver played guitar all night with them in that seedy New Orleans motel room, trading Hank Williams songs and making up new comical verses to Woody Guthrie's "Talkin' Blues" under a fog of whiskey and smoke.

Once you come in contact with the fast-talking Felver he becomes part of your life. His itinerant life-style has earned him more comrades than most mortals could keep track of; but for Felver meeting people is the purpose of living. His Aunt Ceci once told him, "You have friends out there you haven't met yet," and he took this adage to heart. His one challenge to everyone he meets is, "Give me an idea," a request not hard to fulfill from the creative people he regularly encounters.

If there is such a thing as a beatific ethic, Felver personifies it. "Nearly everybody has to live two lives," Robert Frost once noted. Felver, like some combination of coyote and cat, has, at age fifty, lived dozens. He arrived on the San Francisco scene in 1978. It was still a time when the spoken word was celebrated nightly in cafés and bookstores and on the streets. Gregory Corso and Bob Kaufman lived in North Beach; Allen Ginsberg and William Burroughs visited frequently. Ferlinghetti's City Lights Bookstore, the Spaghetti Factory, Keystone Corner, and all of upper Grant Street were stages for readings, performances, and the ongoing discussions that characterized the era. Not long after Lawrence Ferlinghetti met the nonconformist Felver in North Beach, he suggested they journey together to Nicaragua to meet with Ernesto Cardenal, talk politics with the Sandinistas junta, and attend the Ruben Darió poetry festival. The trip resulted in *Seven Days in Nicaragua Libre* (1984), a collaborative photographic memoir published by City Lights Press. By 1984, Felver had completed *West Coast: "Beat & Beyond,"* a one-hour documentary celebrating the life and work of the Beat poets which has become a cult classic. In the mid-1980s, John Cage became smitten with Felver's eclectic style, and it wasn't long before they would collaborate on a short film piece, *John Cage Talks About Cows.* Venturing to New York City in 1985, Felver found Alfred Van Der Marck Editions anxious to publish *The Poet Exposed*, a gallery of contemporary American poets ranging from the Black Mountain group to the New York School.

While he was living in New York in the mid-1980s, a chance introduction to Willem de Kooning ignited Felver's fascination with the art world. Visual artists became the next focus for his camera. In 1987 the American Academy in Rome invited Felver as a visiting artist. "I immediately started working on *Taken by the Romans*, a documentary about the development of contemporary art in 'the eternal city' since World War II." Encouraged by the inclusion of his artist portraits in the 1989 Biennale of Photography in Torino, Felver next traveled the continent photographing major European painters, sculptors, and conceptual artists for an international collection called *The Face of Art* , which parallels the work of the Italian photographer Ugo Mulas. *Regards sur la Generation Beat*, his 1994 photographic and video installation at the Centre Georges Pompidou in Paris, was attended by more than twenty-five thousand people. The same year, Felver internationally screened his hour-long documentary on British sculptor and Turner Prize recipient Tony Cragg. This year PBS will air his documentary *The Coney Island of Lawrence Ferlinghetti.* Blessed with a Nadarian eye for detail, Felver is in constant motion, and the frenetic work never stops. The quest for the next idea propels him "Further," as novelist Ken Kesey once urged his generation.

The photographs in this collection speak to the shared cultural heritage of unrestrained voice and stubborn struggle. Behind every one is the sharp, caring eye of a man whose penchant for great art and social justice converge to form an intimate tribute to the progressive energizers of the human spirit.

Eisenhower Center
Metropolitan College
New Orleans
October, 1995

an · gel (ān´ jəl) *n.* 1. A guardian spirit or guiding influence. 2. A person regarded as good, beautiful, and innocent.

an · ar · chist (ăn´ ər-kĭst) *n.* 1. A person who rejects all forms of coercive control and authority. 2. One who believes in the theory that all forms of authority interfere unjustly with individual liberty.

god (gŏd) *n.* 1. A person or being of supreme value. 2. One that is worshiped, idealized, or highly admired.

ABBIE HOFFMAN
Boulder, Colorado 1983

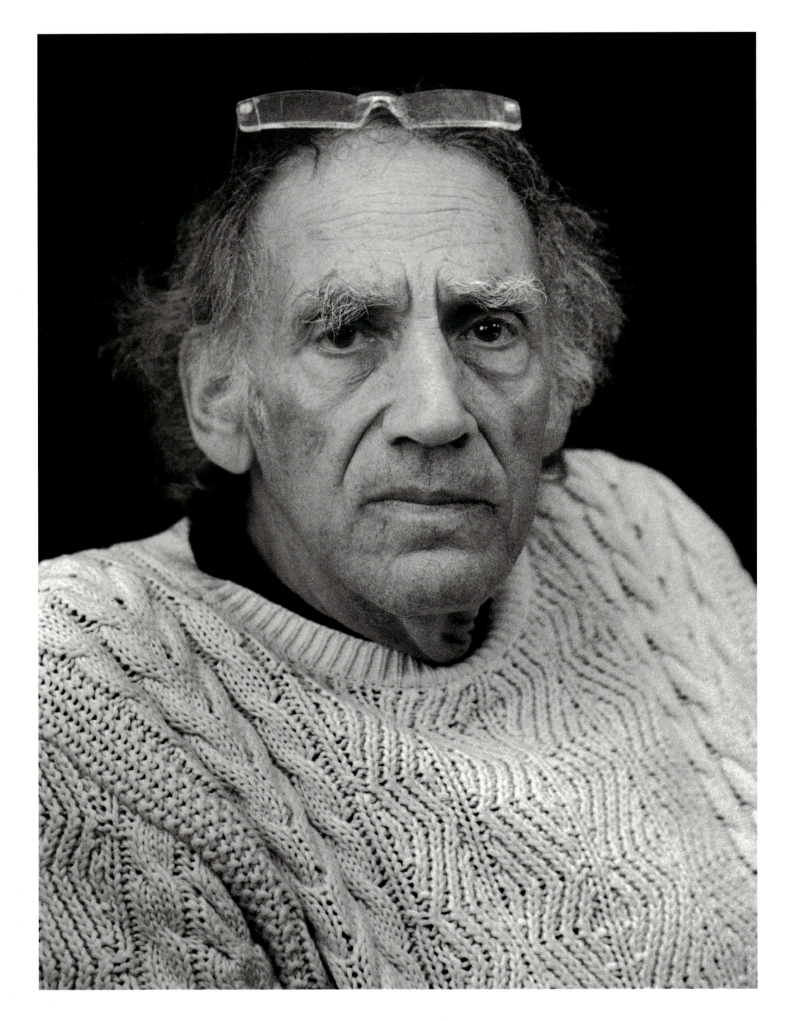

WILLIAM KUNSTLER
New York City 1994

ANGELA DAVIS
Oakland, California 1995

BOBBY SEALE
Philadelphia 1995

JOAN BAEZ
Akron, Ohio 1995

HUNTER S. THOMPSON
Aspen, Colorado 1994

KATHY ACKER
San Francisco 1994

GORE VIDAL
Rome, Italy 1990

NORMAN MAILER
San Francisco 1995

ALLEN GINSBERG
Lowell, Massachusetts 1994

SUSAN SONTAG
New York City 1995

MEREDITH MONK
Boulder, Colorado 1994

ROBERT RAUSCHENBERG
New York City 1991

LOUISE NEVELSON
New York City 1985

JASPER JOHNS
Venice, Italy 1988

MERCE CUNNINGHAM
New York City 1987

JOHN CAGE
New York City 1985

LOUISE BOURGEOIS
New York City 1989

JONAS MEKAS
New York City 1995

ROBERT MOTHERWELL
Greenwich, Connecticut 1989

MARISOL
Venice, Italy 1988

MARK di SUVERO
Long Island City, New York 1985

ISAMU NOGUCHI
Long Island City, New York 1984

JAY McINERNEY
New York City 1994

FRAN LEBOWITZ
New York City 1994

B. B. KING
Atlanta 1994

TONI MORRISON
New York City 1994

ANDREI CODRESCU
New Orleans 1994

GLORIA STEINEM
New York City 1992

KATHRYN
McILHENNY
HIS WIFE
1860 ✠ 1934

MICHAEL T.
PHELAN
1850 ✠ 1895

WILLIAM KENNEDY
Albany, New York 1994

HUBERT SELBY, JR.
San Francisco 1995

KEN KESEY
Berkeley, California 1990

HUGH ROMNEY (WAVY GRAVY)
Berkeley, California 1990

GARY JOHNSTON
San Francisco 1979

BOB KAUFMAN
San Francisco 1982

BOB KAUFMAN, GREGORY CORSO
San Francisco 1982

LAWRENCE FERLINGHETTI
San Francisco 1981

HERBERT AND ARI GOLD
San Francisco 1980

TISA WALDEN, HOWARD HART, GREGORY CORSO, ALLEN GINSBERG, JACK HIRSCHMAN, SARAH MENEFEE
San Francisco 1982

JOHN WIENERS/ROXIE THEATER
San Francisco 1990

GREGORY CORSO, WILLIAM BURROUGHS
San Francisco 1980

ANNE WALDMAN
Boulder, Colorado 1982

PETER ORLOVSKY
San Francisco 1980

TIMOTHY LEARY
San Francisco 1980

IRA COHEN, CAROLINA GOSSELIN
San Francisco 1981

JACK MICHELINE, EDDIE BALCHOWSKY
Guerneville, California 1982

JACK HIRSCHMAN
San Francisco 1993

DIANE di PRIMA
Boulder, Colorado 1982

PHILIP LAMANTIA, HAROLD NORSE
San Francisco 1981

NEELI CHERKOVSKI, RAYMOND FOYE
San Francisco 1980

ALLEN GINSBERG, GREGORY CORSO, WILLIAM BURROUGHS
Boulder, Colorado 1983

ALLEN GINSBERG
San Francisco 1981

WILLIAM BURROUGHS
San Francisco 1980

AL ARONOWITZ
New York City 1994

TED BERRIGAN
Boulder, Colorado 1982

JOHN GIORNO
New York City 1993

HERBERT HUNCKE
New York City 1985

JAMES SCHUYLER / CHELSEA HOTEL
New York City 1985

SEYMOUR KRIM
New York City   1985

SALVATORE SCARPITTA
New York City 1995

JOE BRAINARD
New York City 1985

ROBERT FRANK
New York City 1986

 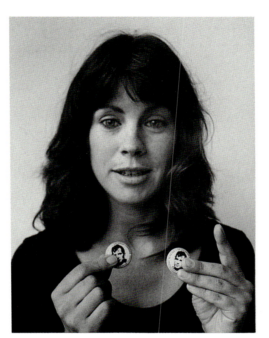 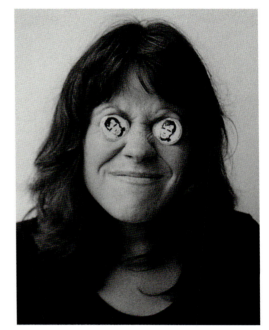

JAN KEROUAC
Boulder, Colorado 1983

RAYMOND FOYE, HERBERT HUNCKE
New York City 1991

WILLIAM BURROUGHS
San Francisco 1980

CAROLYN CASSADY
New York City 1994

MAX AND GREGORY CORSO
San Francisco 1982

NANCY SPERO, LEON GOLUB
New York City 1986

LAURIE ANDERSON
New York City 1985

ROBERT WILSON
Delphi, Greece 1986

DUANE MICHALS
New York City 1986

BRICE MARDEN
New York City 1993

WILLIAM WEGMAN
New York City 1986

RALPH GIBSON
New York City 1992

HELEN FRANKENTHALER
Stamford, Connecticut 1991

ROY LICHTENSTEIN
New York City 1990

FRANK STELLA
New York City 1990

JILL KREMENTZ
New York City 1994

FRED McDARRAH
New York City 1995

WANDA COLEMAN
Berkeley, California 1993

MIGUEL ALGARIN
New York City 1994

ALLAN LANIER, RON KOVIC, JIM CARROLL
New York City 1985

TAYLOR MEAD
New York City 1993

LARRY CLARK
New York City 1986

HETTIE JONES
New York City   1994

TED JOANS
New York City 1985

TED JOANS, CECIL TAYLOR
Brooklyn, New York 1985

RAHSAAN ROLAND KIRK / THE VILLAGE GATE
New York City 1976

AMIRI BARAKA
Newark, New Jersey 1994

NEW YORK CITY
1993

WALTER "HOT LIPS" PAGE, DON CHERRY / VILLAGE VANGUARD
New York City 1986

CECIL TAYLOR, SUN RA
Oakland, California 1991

DIZZY GILLESPIE / FAT TUESDAYS
New York City 1985

PATTI SMITH
New York City 1995

RICK DANKO / LONE STAR CAFE
New York City 1985

PHILIP GLASS
New York City 1991

PHILIP GLASS, ALLEN GINSBERG
Boulder, Colorado 1994

FRANK O'HARA

1926 — 1966

"Grace to be born and live
as variously as possible."

GREEN RIVER CEMETERY
East Hampton, New York 1994

JAN KEROUAC
Lowell, Massachusetts 1994

LARRY RIVERS, KENNETH KOCH
Southampton, New York 1994

LARRY RIVERS
New York City 1984

PORTRAIT OF ALLEN GINSBERG BY ELAINE de KOONING WITH JACK KEROUAC'S PAINT BOX
New York City 1994

WILLEM de KOONING
East Hampton, New York 1985

GEORGE PLIMPTON / ARTISTS & WRITERS BASEBALL GAME
East Hampton, New York 1992

KURT VONNEGUT
Sagaponack, New York 1994

JOHN CAGE
New York City 1985

PETER MATTHIESSEN
Sagaponack, New York 1995

PETER BEARD
Montauk, New York 1995

JULIAN SCHNABEL
Montauk, New York   1995

PAUL MORRISSEY
Montauk, New York 1994

GERARD MALANGA
New York City 1985

NED ROREM
Daytona Beach, Florida 1984

CHARLES HENRI FORD / THE DAKOTA
New York City 1995

BARBARA GUEST
Berkeley, California 1995

JOHN ASHBERY
New York City 1995

ARTHUR MILLER
Woodbury, Connecticut 1994

ROBERT BLY / WALT WHITMAN'S HOME
Huntington, New York 1994

KURT VONNEGUT
Sagaponack, New York 1994

TERRY SOUTHERN
East Canaan, Connecticut 1995

ARLO GUTHRIE
Great Barrington, Massachusetts 1995

PETE SEEGER
Beacon, New York 1995

THE FUGS
Woodstock, New York 1994

SAM AND ANN CHARTERS
Boulder, Colorado 1994

TOWNES VAN ZANDT, RAMBLIN' JACK ELLIOTT
New Orleans 1994

ALICE BROCK
Provincetown, Massachusetts 1994

KINKY FRIEDMAN
Washington, D.C. 1994

TERRY AND JO HARVEY ALLEN
Aspen, Colorado 1984

UTAH PHILLIPS
San Francisco 1995

ROSALIE SORRELS
San Francisco 1995

RICHARD TUTTLE
Abiquiu, New Mexico 1994

RUSSELL MEANS
San Francisco 1996

CHRISTO'S *RUNNING FENCE*
Sonoma, California 1976

ALLEN GINSBERG, GARY SNYDER, DRUMMOND HADLEY
Boulder, Colorado 1982

PAUL KRASSNER
Boulder, Colorado 1983

TIMOTHY LEARY
Boulder, Colorado 1982

PETER ORLOVSKY, ALLEN GINSBERG
Boulder, Colorado 1982

DIANE di PRIMA, ROBERT CREELEY
Boulder, Colorado   1982

TOM CLARK
Berkeley, California 1995

ED AND JENNIFER DORN WITH STAN BRAKHAGE
Boulder, Colorado 1985

KEN KESEY
San Francisco 1995

KEN KESEY'S TWISTER
Boulder, Colorado 1994

DENNIS HOPPER
Los Angeles 1986

OLIVER STONE
Los Angeles 1986

MARIANNE FAITHFULL
San Francisco 1995

SONNY BARGER
Oakland, California 1995

ED KIENHOLZ
Berlin, Germany 1987

KATHY ACKER
San Francisco 1993

CHARLES BUKOWSKI
Los Angeles 1991

HUNTER S. THOMPSON
Aspen, Colorado 1994

STUDS TERKEL
Chicago 1994

MICHAEL McCLURE, RAY MANZAREK / GREAT AMERICAN MUSIC HALL
San Francisco 1991

JIM CARROLL / BROWN HOTEL
Louisville, Kentucky 1994

ALEX CHILTON
New Orleans 1994

JACOB LAWRENCE
Seattle, Washington 1992

THE ZION HARMONIZERS
New Orleans 1994

JIMMY AND ROSALYNN CARTER
Americus, Georgia 1994

MAYA ANGELOU
Oakland, California 1995

JOHN KENNETH AND CATHERINE ATWATER GALBRAITH
Cambridge, Massachusetts 1994

REPRESENTATIVE JOHN LEWIS
Atlanta 1994

ERNESTO CARDENAL, LAWRENCE FERLINGHETTI
Managua, Nicaragua 1984

LAWRENCE FERLINGHETTI
San Francisco 1981

DANIEL BERRIGAN
New York City 1995

JOHN TRUDELL
Los Angeles 1995

CECIL TAYLOR, AMIRI BARAKA
Boulder, Colorado 1994

RITA DOVE
Charlottesville, Virginia 1994

DENISE LEVERTOV
Seattle, Washington 1995

ISHMAEL REED
Oakland, California 1995

ROBERT CREELEY
Paris 1994

RICHARD BRAUTIGAN
San Francisco 1982

SANDRA FISHER, MAX AND R. B. KITAJ
London 1990

DAVID AND DANIEL SHAPIRO
New York City 1992

GEORGE WHITMAN / SHAKESPEARE AND COMPANY
Paris 1990

JEAN-JACQUES LEBEL
Paris 1994

EILEEN MYLES
New York City 1995

DENNIS BANKS
San Francisco 1995

ROBERT DUNCAN
San Francisco 1982

JESS
San Francisco 1994

WILLIAM COLVIG, LOU HARRISON
Aptos, California 1995

JOHN RECHY
Los Angeles 1995

DAVID BROWER
Berkeley, California 1995

ED SANDERS
Woodstock, New York 1995

DAVID AND ADIRA AMRAM
East Hampton, New York 1985

LAWRENCE FERLINGHETTI
Bixby Canyon, California 1985

WILLIAM EVERSON
Davenport, California 1982

GARY SNYDER / KITKITDIZZE
Nevada City, California 1993

PHILIP WHALEN / ZEN CENTER
San Francisco 1993

JOANNE KYGER
Bolinas, California   1993

ARAM SAROYAN
Bolinas, California 1983

ROBERT OLEN BUTLER
New Orleans 1994

W. S. MERWIN
Berkeley, California 1983

CAROLYN KIZER
Sonoma, California 1995

CHARLES AND LINDA BUKOWSKI
Los Angeles 1991

BABA RAM DASS
San Anselmo, California 1995

LAWRENCE FERLINGHETTI
San Francisco 1993

AGNES MARTIN
Taos, New Mexico 1994

ROBERT ARNESON
Benecia, California 1986

RICHARD DIEBENKORN
Healdsburg, California 1992

DAVID HOCKNEY
San Francisco 1985

CLAES OLDENBERG, COOSJE VAN BRUGGEN
New York City 1985

LARRY EIGNER
Berkeley, California 1984

NORMAN MAILER
San Francisco 1995

ANNE WALDMAN, ISHMAEL REED
San Francisco 1994

DAVID BYRNE
Palo Alto, California 1995

Snapped in the past
seen in the present
—fades... fades in the future
—Who knows?
The Pyramids may
dwindle ere

Gregory Corso

for Chris Felver

INDEX OF PHOTOGRAPHS

Acker, Kathy, 7, 147
Algarin, Miguel, 81
Allen, Terry, 127
Allen, Jo Harvey, 127
Amram, Adira, 182
Amram, David, 182
Anderson, Laurie, 69
Angelou, Maya, 157
Arneson, Robert, 196
Aronowitz, Al, 54
Ashbery, John, 115
Baez, Joan, 5
Balchowsky, Eddie, 46
Banks, Dennis, 175
Baraka, Amiri, 89, 164
Barger, Sonny, 145
Beard, Peter, 108
Berrigan, Daniel, 162
Berrigan, Ted, 55
Bly, Robert, 117
Bourgeois, Louise, 18
Brainard, Joe, 61
Brakhage, Stan, 139
Brautigan, Richard, 169
Brock, Alice, 125
Brower, David, 180
Bukowski, Charles, 148, 192
Bukowski, Linda, 192
Burroughs, William, 41, 51,
    53, 65
Butler, Robert Olen, 189
Byrne, David, 203
Cage, John, 17, 106
Cardenal, Ernesto, 160
Carroll, Jim, 82, 152

Carter, Jimmy, 156
Carter, Rosalynn, 156
Cassady, Carolyn, 66
Charters, Ann, 123
Charters, Sam, 123
Cherkovski, Neeli, 50
Cherry, Don, 91
Chilton, Alex, 153
Christo (Running Fence),
    132
Clark, Larry, 84
Clark, Tom, 138
Codrescu, Andrei, 28
Cohen, Ira, 45
Coleman, Wanda, 80
Colvig, William, 178
Corso, Gregory, 36, 39, 41,
    51, 67
Corso, Max, 67
Creeley, Robert, 137, 168
Cunningham, Merce, 16
Danko, Rick, 95
Dass, Baba Ram, 193
Davis, Angela, 3
de Kooning, Elaine (portrait
    of Allen Ginsberg), 102
de Kooning, Willem, 103
di Suvero, Mark, 22
di Prima, Diane, 48, 137
Diebenkorn, Richard, 197
Dorn, Jennifer, 139
Dorn, Ed, 139
Dove, Rita, 165
Duncan, Robert, 176
Eigner, Larry, 200

Elliott, Ramblin' Jack, 124
Everson, William, 184
Faithfull, Marianne, 144
Ferlinghetti, Lawrence, 37,
    160, 161, 183, 194
Fisher, Sandra, 170
Ford, Charles Henri, 113
Foye, Raymond, 50, 64
Frank, Robert, 62
Frankenthaler, Helen, 75
Friedman, Kinky, 126
Fugs, 122
Galbraith, Catherine Atwater,
    158
Galbraith, John Kenneth,
    158
Gibson, Ralph, 74
Gillespie, Dizzy, 93
Ginsberg, Allen, 10, 39, 51,
    52, 97, 102, 133, 136
Giorno, John, 56
Glass, Philip, 96, 97
Gold, Ari, 38
Gold, Herbert, 38
Golub, Leon, 68
Gosselin, Carolina, 45
Green River Cemetery, 98
Guest, Barbara, 114
Guthrie, Arlo, 120
Hadley, Drummond, 133
Harrison, Lou, 178
Hart, Howard, 39
Hirschman, Jack, 39, 47
Hockney, David, 198
Hoffman, Abbie, 1

Hopper, Dennis, 142
Huncke, Herbert, 57, 64
Jess, 177
Joans, Ted, 86, 87
Johns, Jasper, 15
Johnston, Gary, 34
Jones, Hettie, 85
Kaufman, Bob, 35, 36
Kennedy, William, 30
Kerouac, Jack (gravestone),
    99, (paint box), 102
Kerouac, Jan, 63, 99
Kesey, Ken, 32, 140, 141
Kienholz, Ed, 146
King, B. B., 26
Kirk, Rahsaan Roland, 88
Kitaj, Max, 170
Kitaj, R. B., 170
Kizer, Carolyn, 191
Koch, Kenneth, 100
Kovic, Ron, 82
Krassner, Paul, 134
Krementz, Jill, 78
Krim, Seymour, 59
Kunstler, William, 2
Kyger, Joanne, 187
Lamantia, Philip, 49
Lanier, Allan, 82
Lawrence, Jacob, 154
Leary, Timothy, 44, 135
Lebel, Jean-Jacques, 173
Lebowitz, Fran, 25
Levertov, Denise, 166
Lewis, John, 159
Lichtenstein, Roy, 76

McClure, Michael, 151
McDarrah, Fred, 79
McInerney, Jay, 24
Mailer, Norman, 9, 201
Malanga, Gerard, 111
Manzarek, Ray, 151
Marden, Brice, 72
Marisol, 21
Martin, Agnes, 195
Matthiessen, Peter, 107
Mead, Taylor, 83
Means, Russell, 131
Mekas, Jonas, 19
Menefee, Sarah, 39
Merwin, W. S., 190
Michals, Duane, 71
Micheline, Jack, 46
Miller, Arthur, 116
Monk, Meredith, 12
Morrison, Toni, 27

Morrissey, Paul, 110
Motherwell, Robert, 20
Myles, Eileen, 174
Nevelson, Louise, 14
New York City, 90
Noguchi, Isamu, 23
Norse, Harold, 49
O'Hara, Frank (gravestone), 98
Oldenberg, Claes, 199
Orlovsky, Peter, 43, 136
Page, Walter "Hot Lips," 91
Phillips, Utah, 128
Plimpton, George, 104
Rauschenberg, Robert, 13
Rechy, John, 179
Reed, Ishmael, 167, 202
Rivers, Larry, 100, 101
Romney, Hugh (Wavy Gravy), 33

Rorem, Ned, 112
Sanders, Ed, 122, 181
Saroyan, Aram, 188
Scarpitta, Salvatore, 60
Schnabel, Julian, 109
Schuyler, James, 58
Seale, Bobby, 4
Seeger, Pete, 121
Selby, Hubert, Jr., 31
Shapiro, Daniel, 171
Shapiro, David, 171
Smith, Patti, 94
Snyder, Gary, 133, 185
Sontag, Susan, 11
Sorrels, Rosalie, 129
Southern, Terry, 119
Spero, Nancy, 68
Steinem, Gloria, 29
Stella, Frank, 77
Stone, Oliver, 143

Sun Ra, 92
Taylor, Cecil, 87, 92, 164
Terkel, Studs, 150
Thompson, Hunter S., 6, 149
Trudell, John, 163
Tuttle, Richard, 130
Van Bruggen, Coosje, 199
Van Zandt, Townes, 124
Vidal, Gore, 8
Vonnegut, Kurt, 105, 118
Walden, Tisa, 39
Waldman, Anne, 42, 202
Wegman, William, 73
Whalen, Philip, 186
Whitman, George, 172
Wieners, John, 40
Wilson, Robert, 70
Zion Harmonizers, 155